013

Thank you for supporting
Furry Friends, and best
wishes with all your
four-legged "Kids."
        Sincerely,
        Sharon Shoosley

 Mr. Murphy, too!

Butterfly Wings

Two empty nesters' lives are changed forever
when they decide to indulge their canine desires.

Sharon Woosley

Llumina
Press

ISBN: 978-1-60594-822-5 (PB)
        978-1-60594-821-8 (HC)
        978-1-60594-823-2 (EB)

Printed in the United States of America by Llumina Press

Library of Congress Control Number: 2011918669

Acknowledgments

This story is 100 percent true. Most of it comes directly from my memory, as best as I can remember exactly how things happened. Names of non–family members have been changed. But when listing the exact traits of Papillons and coyotes, I did check the following reference materials: Papillons, by Deborah Wood, copyright 2003, by TFH Publications, and Papillons (magazine), Popular Dog Series, volume 40, from editions of Dog Fancy magazine, Bowtie Inc. I also searched the Internet at DogBreedInfo. com and Washington Department of Fish and Wildlife at WDFW.Wa.gov. The rest is either from memory, as I remember it, or pure speculation on my part.

To animals lovers everywhere. May your furry friends bring you much joy and companionship, but most of all, may they give you longevity.

Butterfly Wings

By Sharon Woosley

Chapter One

"Hurry up!" I called back.

My husband, Terry, was several steps behind me. Why couldn't he walk just a little faster? Of course, this wasn't anything new. We walked for exercise and pleasure frequently, usually six miles at a time, sometimes more. Whenever we walked on level, paved surfaces, such as the Salmon Creek Greenway near our home in Vancouver, Washington, I was almost always in the lead. I had to slow down to stay with him. Conversely, he was always ahead of me when we hiked the steep trails of the Columbia Gorge, just twenty miles or so from our house. He would put his head down, hands balled into fists, and deliberately "stomp" up the hills in front of me. For the life of me, I just couldn't seem to keep up.

But today was different. We were not walking for exercise or fitness; this was pure pleasure. We were on the very level sidewalks of Palm Springs, California. And we were on our way to the Fancy Friend, an upscale, and very expensive, pet store in downtown Palm Springs, and I couldn't wait to get there.

I'd had puppy fever for several years, and I finally managed to infect my husband. We had been married for twenty-nine years and had an impressive list of pets we'd owned over the years. If my memory serves me correctly, there were eight dogs, three cats, one batch of five kittens, two parakeets, one rat, two turtles, and oh-so-many tropical fish that had actually been pets at some time. Then there were the two rabbits, one opossum, and a couple of wild birds that we attempted to nurse back to health after they were injured for some reason. (None of them survived, by the way.) And all of those deceased critters were buried on the hillside, next to our garage, along with my mom's dog, because she had no other place to bury him. We had our very own pet cemetery, right on our own property.

We always had several dogs and a couple of cats that resided with us. I let each of our two children have one kitten and one puppy to call their own when they were adolescents. It was always difficult for me, because I wanted to influence them with my choices, but I did manage to let the kids pick out their pets, and name them. Our daughter, Holli, had Pukak the dog and Keesah the cat. Pukak was an American Eskimo, and she actually wrote to the library in Anchorage to find suitable Eskimo names for his pure white color. His official, registered name was Pukak Kannik, which meant "Sugar Snowflake" in Eskimo language. I don't know why she named the cat Keesah; might have just been because she was so young at the time. She was only about four years old when we got the cat from the humane society, and that's what came out when I asked her what we should name her.

Our son, Kyle, was much more mundane with his names: Orlando for the dog (he just liked the sound of it) and Cougar for his cat, because she walked and stalked like a big wild cat. Of course, their pets often ended up being our pals and responsibilities, but we never minded. The kids were just an excuse. We've always loved animals.

We weren't going into the Fancy Friend to actually buy a puppy. No, they were far too expensive here, and we had another week of our stay in the Coachella Valley. It was late November 2004, and we came to celebrate Thanksgiving with my folks, a first in twenty years or so since they had become snowbirds. Kyle was driving out from LA too. We hadn't all been together since last year, and almost never for Thanksgiving.

We were staying in a luxurious time-share, a fringe benefit of a fractional ownership we had purchased on the Oregon Coast years earlier. Pets were not allowed at the time-share, and I wasn't about to let someone else take care of a brand-new puppy. That would be just too much fun to miss out on. Then there was the two-day drive home too. A new puppy on that long of a drive would be difficult to manage. No, we would wait until later—sometime after we got home, maybe even after Christmas. That would be best. Besides, puppies would be much cheaper at home.

But it was always fun to look. I had found this high-end pet store in Palm Springs while surfing the Internet at Mom and Dad's. I was looking into several breeds of dogs to see what would work for us as empty nesters. We (more accurately, *I*) wanted the perfect pooch: something small that could travel with us, didn't need grooming, would be good with kids, didn't bark much, and preferably didn't shed. We had it narrowed down to several possibilities, and there were a couple of them listed for sale at the Fancy Friend.

The Fancy Friend had an interior more like a living room than a pet store. It was small and dimly lit, with only a couple of couches and a few chairs to sit on. The few cages they had were roped off. No pet supplies, no cash register, no signs—just two people to bring out the puppies you wanted to see. They had four or five different breeds. One was a Havenese, which was the one I fell in love with on the Internet. I think there were a pug and a Yorkie, but they were already doled out to other clients in the store. So we asked to see the Havenese, and they instructed us to sit down, relax, and enjoy the encounter.

We did as instructed, and of course instantly fell in love. He was the sweetest little white fluff ball, who quickly cuddled into the space between Terry and me and fell asleep. We petted, cooed, and stroked him for about ten minutes, before they asked to put him back in his cage. Now, I'm sure, that at this point, most people are hooked, reeled in, and filleted. But we were going to be different. We weren't actually there to buy, only to look. We asked to see another, but by this time the owners had figured us out and said that the puppies were tired and needed to rest. We left, albeit reluctantly. We really did have puppy fever. We just had to wait awhile for the cure.

A few nights later, we went to the Palm Springs Street Fair, one of my favorite activities. It is a weekly outdoor market where the main street is closed at 5:00 p.m. and a variety of vendors spread their wares for several blocks. They sell everything from local produce, to art, to jewelry, to you-name-it. There is usually food and live entertainment as well. Pets are welcome too, and it's always a great time to people-watch and admire the dogs.

I had been considering puppies and breeds for months. The finalists for our perfect pooch were a Pug, an Italian Greyhound, a Papillon, and a Miniature Schnauzer. I eliminated the Havenese based on the grooming he would need. I had been considering the choices for months, and I couldn't put the final four in any particular order. They were all wonderful. But that night, at the street fair, I looked over and saw a beautiful, obedient, tiny, brown-and-white Papillon, and instantly, my decision was made. I wanted a Papillon.

Chapter Two

The Papillon breed has a long and colorful history of being a favorite of humans. In fact, Papillons were so popular with European royals in the 1500 and 1600s, it has been rumored that it was actually made illegal for commoners to own them! You could only possess a Papillon if you were a royal. Many ancient paintings picture French royals with their dainty and loyal canine companions. A particularly famous one pictures Louis XIV with all of his rather large family. But his playful Papillon seems to take center stage, leaving one to wonder if the dog isn't the most important family member.

Other famous people who owned a Papillon were King Henry III, Madame de Pompadour, and Marie Antoinette. Some stories of how these little dogs impacted the lives of their royal masters still survive to this day. One odd tale is of King Henry III, who owned several of the prized animals. One day when a monk arrived at his home to deliver a letter, one of his Papillons pitched a fit and would have nothing to do with the stranger. It turned out the little dog was right. The monk proved to be a traitor who later stabbed the king, and he ultimately died of his wounds.

But probably the most famous story that survives today is that of Marie Antoinette. There are several versions around, but it is generally reported that she kept several Papillons, and she loved them so much, she carried one with her to the guillotine. All accounts agree that Marie did not survive, but the dog did. One, probably exaggerated, version even says that the hooded executioner took the dog home and loved it for the rest of its life . . . but then how could he if he was but a commoner?

Some modern-day celebrities who own Papillons are Lauren Bacall, Leo Laporte, George Takei, and Christina Aguilera.

So what makes up this little gem of a K-9 companion? Its breeding history is so long, much of the very early crossbreeding has been lost. But some say early ancestors were mixed with small dogs from Asia. Others say it is strictly the miniaturization of another breed called the Continental toy spaniel. Still others say the royals fell in love with a blend of several different lap-sized dogs and those Continental toys. But there is general agreement among experts that those early Continental toy spaniels were probably the largest contributing gene pool for what today is known as Papillons, Cavalier King Charles Spaniels, and English Toy Spaniels.

The standard look for the Papillon breed is a mostly white body, with black, brown, or reddish patches over the ears, and scattered around the back and tail. If the dog has brown *and* black patches, it is known as a tricolor. To be show dogs, Papillons also must have a white blaze down their forehead and cannot have white on their ears. Their tail is long and curves up over their back, like a squirrel's tail. But it has long hair that forms a beautiful silky "plumage" that hangs down nearly a foot. Paps have long slender noses, bright round eyes that do not bulge from the head like Chihuahuas', long legs, and dainty, perfectly shaped little paws. In fact, their perfect proportions are what I love most about the Papillons. In my mind, they look something like a tiny collie.

Although there is no official distinction in the names, such as a toy or standard, Papillons do come in several sizes. Most can range from eight to twelve inches tall and be between seven and fourteen pounds, but I have seen a few that are even bigger than this. They have long delicate fur that resembles human hair, shed less than other dogs, and don't have the usual doggie odor.

There are two types of Papillons. One is called a Phalène, which is French for "moth." The ears of this type hang down, move freely, and resemble the closed wings of a moth. These dogs particularly resemble those spaniels of yesteryear. The other type is just known as the Papillon, which is French for "butterfly." This one has large ears that stand up erect and have long wisps of hair, or fringe, that grow from the ears. When they grow mature, their ears resemble the outline of a beautiful swallowtail butterfly, especially when viewed from behind the head. It takes about three years for the full ear fringe to fill in and make that distinctive butterfly look. In the meantime, Papillons are funny-looking little critters whose ears seem to be too big for their tiny bodies.

This was the type of Papillon I wanted. The Phalène dogs were cute, but to me, just not nearly as attractive or amazing as the "butterflies." The butterfly-eared versions were much more endearing to me, and I was hopelessly drawn to them. My mind was made up, and there would be no changing it. I was hooked on the Papillon. Terry would just have to adjust.

All the books and articles I found said that Papillons are a wonderful breed. That they are good with kids, can handle long walks or be content on the couch, are good travelers, faithful and loving companions, and even good guard dogs. What? How could something that tiny be a guard dog? The books said that the breed is so intelligent, that it is alert to changes in its environment, and will let its master know when something is wrong or different, but then settle back into its routine when things return to normal. They also said that they learn quickly and are easy to train . . . except for housebreaking. Well, I chose to ignore that little tidbit and moved right along with my decision. (But it turned out they were right.)

Papillons are great, loving, and faithful companions. They want to be with you every minute, whether you are walking, sleeping, painting, cooking, or doing the laundry. They will stare at you all day, with those ears up, hoping you will notice and give them some attention. They are the happiest when they are closest to you.

Yes, there were a few possibilities of negative traits as well: excessive barking, shyness, and possible nipping. But the dog I chose would have none of these nasty habits. I'd make sure of that with love and proper training. Ha!

Chapter Three

Our drive home from Southern California was pleasant, as usual. We enjoyed traveling by car. It gave us time to talk, time to nap, scenery to enjoy, and an excuse to eat fast food. Several times along the thousand-mile-plus journey, our conversation turned to puppies.

Though he was excited too, Terry had graciously given me the privilege of single-handedly choosing our next dog. We had two grown children, and we were empty nesters now. Our son, Kyle, had transferred to a college in Los Angeles several years earlier and, even after graduation, never bothered to come back. He'd fallen in love with LA, and a certain girl who lived there. Holli, our daughter, was now twenty-seven and had moved out a couple of years earlier and taken Pukak with her. She had a significant other, who had custody of his two young children too. Even though they lived close by, we didn't see much of them because they were busy living their new life together.

All of our other old animals had passed away, except for Cougar. She was our son's kitten, but now she was seventeen, and we knew she couldn't be around much longer. We decided, when she was gone, we would not get any more cats. Eventually, we wanted to travel, or at least be snowbirds like my mom and dad, and we didn't know what we would do with a cat while we were away for long periods of time. A small dog we would just pick up and take with us.

Not everyone agreed with our desire for a puppy. Several people said they were too much work, or too much responsibility. Some said they had reached the age where they would prefer to travel without the worry of what to do with a dog. My own mother thought I was crazy.

"What about your new carpets?" she asked. Hmmm, although they weren't technically brand-new, it was a valid issue.

"And it hurts too much to lose them," she added.

"Well, that is tough. But I think that the pain of losing an old friend is worth the lifetime of love I get in return,"

I said. "I don't want to miss out on years of love, to spare myself the pain of loss." She did not necessarily agree.

As I mentioned, we always had several pets. The day we got married, we had three dogs. I had two Miniature Poodles, and Terry had a larger dog, which was half collie and half Samoyed. Both of us let our animals sleep with us when we were single. It was quite amusing to see all five of us attempt to sleep in the same bed when we got married. Within a few nights, all pets were relegated to beds of their own, and all was well again. Over the years, three cats came and several dogs came and went. Keesah died at the age of sixteen, quietly, in our garage. It was apparent that Cougar would probably do the same. Most of the dogs died from old age, though one got hit by a car and one disappeared. Our daughter still had Pukak, but he too was getting pretty old and a little decrepit. Since he was with her, he wasn't our responsibility. We just had to doggy-sit him on occasion.

We had to put Orlando down just before our trip to California. He was enduring multiple problems and started having seizures, so we made the difficult decision to end his suffering. He was our last canine companion, so it was difficult for us to come home to an empty house, no wagging tails or sloppy kisses. Sure, the old cat was happy we finally came home to serve her, but still, it seemed lonely, and we realized this was a turning point for us. It was time for *us*. Time to put what *we* wanted ahead of everything else.

We wanted a dog that we could pick up and take with us, wherever we went. We walked several miles a week and hiked frequently during the summers, and we wanted one that would enjoy going with us. I also wanted one that wouldn't need grooming, didn't bark, was good with kids, and wasn't hyper. I didn't think that was too much to ask! Before our trip, I purchased a dog encyclopedia and also searched the Internet extensively. I stuck with my decision to get a Papillon. End of discussion.

Chapter Four

We got married September 6, 1975. It seems a bit odd to admit it now, but he picked me up in a bar. It didn't feel shameful at the time. But now I do wince a bit when I tell people the story, since we rarely visit bars anymore. Oh well, it has given us more than a few chuckles over the years, and the marriage seems to have worked out OK.

I was twenty-three, and Terry was thirty. He had been married before and was heartbroken when he realized it had been a huge mistake. His first wife did not want children, so he was anxious to start a family with me, as soon as I was ready. Holli was born in the spring of 1977, and Kyle followed in 1979. We spent the next two decades raising kids and participating in all the activities that come with it: soccer at many levels, homework, music lessons, T-ball, baseball, basketball, coaching, sleepovers, 4-H Dog Club, parades, camping, travels, jobs, friends, dances, colleges, and graduations—just to name a few. We always put the kids first. Our own needs and desires took a backseat to theirs, and now it was over. We were empty nesters. It seemed that the kids had come along, and the decades had spun by in a whirling flash. Where did all those years go?

We'd always enjoyed a good solid marriage. Of course we had our occasional spats, and some ups and downs, like most couples. But overall, even though we got married less than a year after meeting each other, we turned out to be pretty compatible. We were generally of the same mind when it came to all the major topics: politics, religion, finances, family, discipline. In fact, we discussed these topics in detail when we were considering getting married. But surprisingly, we did not discuss the love of animals. I guess since we both had pets, it didn't seem to be an issue. But I'm grateful it turned out that both of us love animals, because it is a very big issue to me now. And I don't know if we would have survived the years if he told me I could not have pets. It might have had the same effect as his first wife saying he couldn't have kids!

The truth is, Terry usually made most of our major decisions. Oh, yeah sure, he always *said* he let me decide. But in the end, it was usually his choice that won out. Whether we were choosing furniture, cars, paint colors, or what to have for dinner, he usually made the final decision. It wasn't that he consciously tried to, he simply couldn't help himself.

This time, as a sort of compensation for all those times I had complained about him overruling my choices, he said I could pick the new dog. Completely my choice. He said he wouldn't try to influence me at all, that he would accept my choice and not say a word. Well, I was determined to make him stick to his promise. So far he had, and my choice was a Papillon!

We got back into town on Sunday evening, and Monday was spent on settling back into the usual routine and catching up on mail and chores. By Tuesday, however, I had time to read the morning paper again. Sure enough, there was an ad: Papillon Puppies, $425. Terry said I should call. I put it off knowing that if I did, we would probably have a new puppy.

He asked me again an hour later if I called (like I would have been able to keep it a secret if I did!). I said no, and he accepted that. But when he asked me again at noon, I couldn't resist any longer.

I called the number, and the nice lady told me there were four to choose from and gave me directions. I said I had to work until three and wouldn't be able to get there until at least four thirty or so, as it was an hour drive from my home, and I had to get home from work first. Her name was Doris, and she said that would be fine. So we agreed to meet then.

Of course, where we live, 4:00 p.m. is the middle of heavy rush hour, and we had to travel right through the thick of the traffic. It took us an extra half hour because of the traffic. I was anxious to get there, but on the way, I agonized over how I would pick just one from the litter of four. What would help me decide? How could I narrow down the choice? Would "the one" choose me? I heard they could. Well, I didn't need to worry. In the four hours since I called, Doris had sold three of the puppies. I looked into that real-life baby playpen and saw the tiniest, cutest, little brown-and-white puppy I had ever seen in my life and said, "I'll take him." No questions asked.

Chapter Five

It took about a half hour to fill out the paperwork, get instructions on toy-sized-puppy care, and head back home again . . . another hour drive in good conditions. Of course, we were heading right back into that same rush-hour traffic. Our total trip took nearly four hours to travel about sixty miles round-trip! But we didn't care. We were in love—pure puppy love. I was happy that I didn't have to drive and could hold and cuddle my new little ball of puppy fur. I felt a little sorry for Terry that he couldn't.

To get our mind off the traffic, we immediately began trying on names for our new little guy. I had several in mind and put them all out for Terry to consider. After trying a few, he said he kind of liked *Baxter*, and I said, "OK. Baxter it is."

We got Baxter home and immediately took digital pictures of him so we could send them to our family and friends in far-off, distant places . . . like California! We told my parents that they had a new grandchild, and our son that he had a new little brother. Of course, that was met with objections from him. He didn't want to be demoted to second place!

Baxter was just seven weeks old when we brought him home. He was a fluffy white fur ball, with big brown bandit-type patches over his eyes and ears and a brown sidesaddle patch. His tail seemed kind of short, but it curled up over his back anyway and dug a deep rut in his soft puppy fur. Sometimes it looked as if it was made for a hook, and we could have hung him up by it. Of course it was much too flexible for that, but it looked solid at first glance. He had big, bright, deep brown eyes, with no tearstains, and a pink-and-black-speckled nose. His ears were, of course, his most commanding feature, as with all Papillons. They must have stood up three or four inches from his forehead. And between those ears, and those big brown eyes, you always knew exactly what he was thinking.

Baxter slept a lot, on my lap, of course. But when he wasn't sleeping, he would run and play with gleeful joy: jumping, playing tug-of-war, and trying his best to dig the spots out of the kitchen linoleum. Cougar tolerated him, but she wasn't much interested in him. Occasionally, she would give us a dirty look, as if to ask us why we were doing this to her. And he seemed to understand: cats weren't much fun.

We bought him a nice doggie bed and kept it in the bathroom. We chose the bathroom because it had a door so we could close him in, we could heat it with a small space heater, and it had vinyl flooring . . . ever mindful of those carpets! Eventually, he would sleep with us, but not until he was fully house-trained. I just didn't realize at that time how long that would take.

We also took him to our regular veterinarian within a few days. We wanted to have him microchipped, in case he was ever lost or stolen, as well as to give him a general checkup. As part of his care and feeding instructions, Doris told me to give him Karo syrup twice a day to keep his blood sugar up. She explained that toy breed puppies are so small that they need a little extra boost to stay healthy. I had never heard of that, so I wanted to check with the vet to make sure. She agreed. In fact, she said, "Most definitely."

The vet also found that he had ear mites and a mild eye infection. So for the next six weeks, Baxter and I spent much quality time feeding and medicating at least every day. He was the cutest and most cooperative little patient I ever had. We bonded each time I had to administer his medications, and I grew to cherish that time we spent together. He loved the Karo syrup, so I used it as a reward after he endured the drops in his eyes and ears. He knew that medications meant something yummy would follow, and he did not resist a bit. When we were done, he almost always curled up in my lap for a nap—apparently no hard feelings. He was just so precious. I guess it was my age, but I couldn't help myself. He tugged at my heartstrings like no other pet I had ever owned.

It was not long before it was time to think of Christmas and start the many preparations. He couldn't understand why we were bringing that *huge* tree into our home, and why we kept chasing him away from those pretty packages underneath it. They just looked like so much fun! But despite being a newborn, in a new environment, torn away from his mother and siblings, and getting scolded for constantly being under foot during the many activities and visitors of the season, Baxter adjusted quickly. He seemed to love being with us as much as we loved having him, and we all bonded deeply and completely.

Baxter was so small, and so cute. He created a commotion everywhere we went. He was about the size of a baby rabbit, and nearly fit in the palm of my hand. A few days after we got him, we went to the pet store to buy him a collar, but nothing would fit. He was too small for even the shortest dog collar, so we had to buy him a ferret collar. It was the only thing that fit him snug enough to not slide off over his head. It was Christmas red and had a tinkly little bell on it, perfect for the season. And for the next five or six months, until he finally outgrew the collar, I could hear him wherever he was because of that little bell.

Soon after the first of the year, we put him on a leash and took him out for his first walk. We wanted to get him used to going for walks and being on a leash. What better way than just to let him grow up that way.

The weather was frigid. It was about forty degrees, and the wind was howling. Our first walk was along a gravel path, next to a golf course. Despite the weather, there were several people walking there, and we couldn't go very far before someone would stop us to admire Baxter. One woman jogged to catch up with us, then was too out of breath to speak. It was absolutely delightful. It was the first of many, many times I was to hear the question

"What kind of dog is that?" And then explain about the ears that, when mature, would make a beautiful outline of butterfly wings. And translate the word "papillon" from French to English.

We didn't stay long at the walking path that day because Baxter got too cold. When he began shivering hard, we left to get him inside. Of course I willingly took on the difficult job of cuddling him to get him warm again. Not long after that, we took him out and bought him a sweater so we could walk longer. The sweater, of course, made him even more of a curiosity, and he drew even greater attention when he wore it.

A couple of weeks later, when he was headed back to the vet for his next set of vaccination shots, we caused a minor traffic jam while walking across the parking lot. He looked too small and out of proportion to be on a leash. A lady stopped her car, rolled down the window, and said, "Is that a dog?" She drawled it out and spoke slowly as if in total disbelief. Apparently, she had a difficult time accepting he was really a dog.

"Yep. He is." I chuckled. She just stared and slowly said, "Wow." Meanwhile, all the cars trying to turn into the lot got jammed up behind her. It was fun to watch. Baxter loved all the attention, and so did I. He seemed to enjoy meeting people, and kids. He always greeted them with plenty of wags and doggie kisses, whether they approved or not.

Chapter Six

We lived on two acres just three miles from the northern edge of town, but it felt like seventy or eighty acres in the country. We purchased the property and had the house built twenty-five years earlier. The only change we had seen during that time was that the owners of the two neighboring parcels, approximately forty acres each, had logged their land about ten years earlier. Not much else had changed since we'd moved there—no construction, no growth, no commercial.

Nothing was done to finish off those eighty acres after the logging was finished and the slash burned, so it just grew into a wild field. There were good-sized alder trees that had grown up in the ten years, and some grass, but blackberries and thistles had just about taken over. Terry used the riding lawn tractor to cut a narrow path that ran away from the house, and down toward a creek, oh maybe a couple hundred yards. We walked it occasionally, but you had to be careful not to snag a blackberry vine, or step on a thistle.

Our property didn't go more than a few feet before hitting the line that marked a new parcel, but since no one used the large vacant land for anything, that line was kind of blurred, and we used it all the time. It was kind of a fringe benefit. We always remarked how nice it was to have the privacy and use the space, but not have to pay taxes on it.

It was this vacant, but nearby space that we designated "the potty spot." All our dogs used it over the decades. It was far enough away from our deck space that we didn't even need to pick up poop, yet close enough for them to go out and come right back. We had a nice large flat yard in the back and the balance of the two acres out our front door. But most of the time, all of our dogs went right over the property line and did their business. It was very convenient and had worked for twenty-five years.

This is where we began taking Baxter for housebreaking. We would carry him out there, put him down, and call him back when he was finished. We always stayed with him, but he was so small he would go into or under the bushes to sniff around to see who else had been there. Sometimes I would worry that he would get stuck in there, and I didn't know how I would get him out, but it never happened. He loved exploring, but always came out on his own. Once in a while, he wouldn't come back when I would call him. Then, I would have to go after him and carry him back inside with a "stern" scolding, followed by lots of love, of course.

Terry was a "paperboy." He was responsible for getting the largest newspaper in the metro area from the printing press to the customer. He had about 1,500 customers, who were delivered by seven or eight adult carriers every night. He had worked for the paper for about thirty-five years—longer than we had known each other. But for most of our married lives, I owned and operated our Baskin Robbins store. Both jobs were considered self-employment and left us with comparatively small hours and fairly flexible schedules.

I had a steady parade of teenaged employees who were always interesting, to say the least. Some were good employees, some not so much. And some wanted (or needed) a friendly relationship with me, the boss. It just happened that at this time, I had a very sweet high schooler, named Liz, who got a puppy about the same time I got Baxter. The dogs were close to the same age, and we spent way too much time comparing our new little treasures. She had actually gone to the same breeder's home I had, looking for the perfect pup. But she wanted a miniature dachshund, and Doris didn't have any at that time. We were both shocked to find we had come very close to getting a puppy from the same place, at the same time. But Liz did find her mini "doxie" and named her Bonnie—her boyfriend already had Clyde . . . too cute!

There was a veterinary office in the same plaza as my store, and I had been taking my dogs to them for years. One day, Baxter was due for his next puppy shots, so I took him with me to work. He couldn't come into the store, of course—that was against the Health Department's rules—but he could stay in the car, and Terry could pick him up when he joined me for lunch.

When Liz arrived for her shift, she called her dad and had him bring Bonnie to the store so she could meet Baxter. Her dad must have been an animal lover too, since he was only too happy to oblige and was there in a matter of minutes. I was so used to Baxter's dainty and petite little silhouette that Bonnie seemed huge and bloated to me, sort of like a glove that had been jokingly inflated. Just a short neck and short little legs sticking out of that short little round body. Of course, she was still very small, but looked much different from Baxter. Even Liz's dad remarked about how strange it was to have her look so large, that most everyone always remarked about how small she was. It was loads of fun, and I enjoyed every minute of the encounter. The pups enjoyed it too.

A few weeks later, Bonnie developed a severe hernia in that round little tummy, and Liz was worried sick about her. I completely understood. I didn't know how anybody could love an animal so much, and losing that little ball of puppy fur would be more than I could take. Liz quit shortly after that, and I never knew what happened to Bonnie. Did she mend and heal OK? Or did the unthinkable happen? Guess I will never know, but then maybe I don't want to.

When Baxter was about three or four months old, he developed a very peculiar habit. Now, I know, most people wouldn't talk much about their pets' urinating. And usually, that would be appropriate. But of course Baxter was different, and it didn't take long for him to become an even greater star because of it. You see, he didn't urinate like any dog I had ever had before. No, it wasn't because he squatted, rather than lift his leg. It wasn't because he tried to reach the biggest trees, or fire hydrants, or anything like that. You see, Baxter stood on his *front* legs and walked around in a six-foot circle to relieve himself! His little behind and tail would bob and bounce around, up there in the air, while he was making his circle. It was hilarious. And it was the hit of all our family and friends. Everybody wanted us to "make him do his thing."

I would watch him when he was outside and chuckle at his strange antics. But when I found those six-foot circles in the living room or dining room, on our still-fairly-new carpets, it wasn't so funny, and I remembered Mom's warning.

Chapter Seven

Around the first of February, I decided it was time for puppy kindergarten. I signed us up at a local pet store, and we were off. Baxter loved it from the start. All those new people to meet . . . and dogs too? He thought it was just too much fun and was in absolute puppy heaven!

We had a fairly large class. There was Barkly the beagle, Bently the basset, Chuck the black Lab, Susy the German shepherd, Chewie the mix, and a few nondescript others. Of all the dogs in the class, Baxter was, by far, the smallest and the most outgoing. Any of those dogs could have picked him up and tossed him like a rag doll. Fortunately, our trainer, Debbie, kept pretty good control of the entire group. But in every class session for six weeks, Baxter stole the show.

He loved being in class but, like my human children, thought school was much better spent on fun stuff than on actual learning. He was extremely smart, but just didn't want to take the time to do what he was supposed to do. He would rather sniff around, play with his leash, entice another student to play, or draw a store customer over to pet him. After the first lesson, the trainer told me that I should take him home and work with him . . . lots. That he needed a lot of disciplining. Duh! Like I didn't know that.

But I did work with him whenever I could, and he managed to learn "sit," "stay," "down," "drop it," and "leave it," though it took hours of work. For our final, our assignment was to learn a trick and surprise Debbie. I taught him to roll over, and she loved it, but she failed him anyway—said he needed more discipline. Oh well. At least I didn't have to face the PTA.

Within just a few months after bringing Baxter home, Cougar died. She just slowly faded away on the couch. It was like having the batteries die on a flashlight and watching the light slowly dim to nothing. I offered her milk and tuna every day, but mostly she wasn't interested. She was eighteen years old and I knew she was dying. I think Baxter did too; he seemed to understand and didn't bother her. When she did finally pass away, we let him smell her while she was still warm. He just sat down beside her and looked at her with those ears perked up and his little head cocked to one side. They were not fast friends to one another, but I'm certain that somehow he understood she was gone. Losing her was sad, but I was secure in knowing she had lived a good long life, and that is all you can ask of a four-footed friend.

So now it was just the three of us.

About this same time, Terry somehow discovered that Baxter loved beer. A dog after his own heart! Whenever Terry opened a bottle (always Budweiser; never a microbrew for him), Baxter was right there, in his face. He would lick the excess beer from Terry's mustache after Terry took a swig. It didn't take long for Terry to leave an extra little bit there for him and even, on occasion, give him a couple of drops in the bottle cap. Always over my protests. But it made Terry proud to show everyone that despite his size, Baxter was a "man's dog." Aarrrrrrr! And he was very careful with it; he never gave him much, so I didn't interfere. In fact, it was fun to see how much they both enjoyed the game.

It was spring now, and we were walking frequently. He had learned to walk on the leash without problems, and we took him everywhere—to gas stations, grocery stores, and restaurants—though he had to stay in the car in those places. He had won over several bank employees, and they always gave him a milk bone when we did business with them. He was a big hit at the antique mall. We had items for sale there, and the owners would never allow us to just slip in and out. We always had to bring Baxter in for a visit and a chat. We never forced him on anyone if they weren't interested. But we proudly took him to the homes and offices of those who didn't mind, and on all of our walks, whether they were long or short. We got just as much fun out of the attention as Baxter did.

He did hike with us in the Columbia Gorge, near Portland, Oregon, several times. I think his record was seven miles in one day. But mostly these days, we only had time to walk along level trails near our home. The one we frequented the most was Salmon Creek Greenway. It was paved and mostly level, and a six-mile round-trip. Sometimes we walked all six miles; other times we only had time for part of it. But the three of us became a common site along the path.

He had grown into an attractive dog with beautiful markings, and he continued to garner attention from dog lovers and others everywhere. Always, they asked, "What kind of a dog is that?" Explaining to them about him and his butterfly wings was pure joy, and I never grew tired of telling it.

Chapter Eight

Often, we saw the same people in the same places, walking with their dogs. We humans didn't know each other's names, but we knew the dogs' names. Baxter always recognized the golden labradoodle, and the labradoodle recognized him. They would exchange hello sniffs, then wags, then move along. Sometimes I would stand and exchange doggie tales with the anonymous owners for twenty or thirty minutes. It was more than just exercise for me, it was entertainment.

Baxter loved children too. Whenever he could, he would run up to them with the eagerness of a hound on the scent. Little girls especially seem to be drawn to small dogs and would ask if they could pet him. It was difficult to say no, when he was already bouncing on his hind feet, trying to give them several of his happy doggie kisses. It was great fun to see their reactions, and I was having a ball.

Also, around April or May, he was released from sleeping alone in his bathroom prison and joined us in the bedroom. Rather, I should say, in our bed.

As I've said, Terry and I each had dogs that slept with us. But for both of us, whether as a couple, or in our single lives, the dogs always slept *on* the bed, and usually at our feet. Even the cats slept on the bed, but near our heads. Not so Baxter. It seemed he had to do everything differently.

Now that he was five or six months old, he had proven that he could make it through the night without needing to potty. So I was ready to invite him to join us instead of being shut into the bathroom. One night, he trudged into the bathroom, crawled in his bed, took a deep sigh, and looked up at me, as if to say "Good night, Mommy." He was surrendering to his lonely fate for the night. I couldn't take it anymore, and I checked with Terry to make sure it would be OK. Then we both asked him if he wanted to sleep with us. He couldn't believe his good fortune.

"Really?" he said with those eyes and ears.

"Come on!" I said. And he happily followed me through the door, raced up the stairs, and got to the bedroom before me. I picked him up and put him on the bed because he was too small to make the jump. Then I crawled in and settled down for a nice long sleep. Terry and I played with him a bit since it was the first time we were all together at bed time. After a short while, he lay down, and I thought, OK, here we are—one little happy family. But just before I drifted off, I felt this gentle little scratching on my shoulder. Scratch, scratch, scratch. I ignored it at first, not knowing what he wanted. But he kept it up. Scratch, scratch, scratch. He was very patient with me. Scratch, scratch, scratch. I finally lifted the covers, and he dove under like a rocket. He wanted to sleep *under* the covers, not on them!

That was the first time I experienced really sleeping with my pet, and I can't tell you how good it felt. When he would crawl under the covers, curl up next to my legs, take a big deep sigh, and fall asleep, it told me all was right in the world, and that he loved me as much as I loved him. It was a great comfort to me. We all slept together from then on, under the covers, happy to be together.

It's difficult to admit, but we enjoyed spoiling him and were guilty of buying him too many toys and gifts. We both enjoyed surprising him with some new little thing. It seemed he had more toys than our own children had when they were growing up. I exercised discipline with them, but couldn't seem to find the strength with Baxter. Terry bought him a talking Taco Bell Chihuahua at a garage sale for twenty-five cents one time, and it was one of his favorite toys. He would grab it in his mouth, trot around the room with it, and trigger the voice mechanism over and over and over. Eventually, it could barely be heard because the battery was nearly dead, but he loved it anyway. And we always got a chuckle out of hearing him make it say, "Yo quiero Taco Bell!" "Yo quiero Taco Bell!" "Yo quiero Taco Bell!"

Also, as a human joke, I bought him a small red cement fire hydrant once, on a trip to the beach. I thought all spoiled little dogs should have their very own fire hydrant. He didn't get the joke, or use the hydrant much (it's hard to hit a hydrant while walking on your front feet), but our friends thought it was hilarious, and it was always a topic of conversation when they saw it.

Chapter Nine

We spent the next year or so walking, partying, traveling, and sleeping together. He was always the center of attention, wherever we were, whether he deserved it or not. When our daughter got married in August 2005, we had the rehearsal and after-party in our backyard, and of course he stole the show. I put my mother in charge of watching after him, and kept him on a leash to make it easier for her. The children in attendance loved him, and so did most of the rest of the guests. I believe he got at least as much attention as the bride and groom, maybe more. Sorry, Holli and Jeff!

Shortly after the wedding, my brother's girlfriend, Janae, had a birthday party for her Chihuahua, named Chico. He was turning three, and she had given him a party each year. She didn't invite people to his parties though, only dogs. But their owners could stay for the fun if they wanted. She always served tacos and margaritas for the people, and a peanut butter and doggie-treat cake for the dogs.

We had teased her over the years about Chico's other parties, because she didn't invite our old dog, Orlando. She said he was too old, and too big to party with the little guys. We told her we had to pay for months of therapy for Orlando, because he had suffered severe emotional trauma for being rejected and left out. She would laugh and tell us to just send her the bill. But Orlando was gone now, and Baxter had made the cut. He managed to garner an invitation to *the* K-9 social event of the year. I thought the whole idea was just too cute, and was happy to be included.

There were four little dogs at the party; the other three were Chihuahuas. One of the long-haired ones even looked enough like Baxter to be a sibling, but of course they were not related. I could then understand why so many people asked me if Baxter was a longhaired Chihuahua, and tried to be a little less insulted.

All of the other dogs, including Chico, hung back and acted a bit uncertain, or shy. They stayed pretty close to their owners. Not so Baxter. He played with Chico's toys, ate his food, visited all the partygoers, and licked the birthday cake all by himself. He did not care that it was Chico's party, let him cry if he wanted . . . Baxter had a blast!

Chapter Ten

We traveled back to Palm Springs for several weeks the next Christmas, and naturally, Baxter went with us. He wasn't allowed in the time-shares where we stayed, but my mother was happy to keep him during those times, and my dad loved walking him around the senior park where they lived. On Christmas morning, he helped me hand out the presents under the tree. Then, he helped me open mine. He was such a little helper! Actually, just plain nosey was more like it. He always had to be in the middle of everything. To Terry's dismay, I even dressed him up in a Santa Paws suit and paraded him around that senior park on Christmas Day. He said he was embarrassed for Baxter, being a man's dog and all. The suit was very warm for him in that climate, but Terry shouldn't have worried. Baxter thoroughly enjoyed having all those little old ladies fussing over him . . . too warm or not.

We made a point to stay in motels where pets were welcome whenever we traveled, and it was always a joy to have him with us. Always explaining about those ears . . . about those butterfly wings . . . and about that French word. Somehow, in our old age, we empty nesters had managed to make a family again, thanks to Baxter. It was great fun, and all three of us were having the time of our lives.

And as all puppies do, he had a knack for bringing everyone closer together. My parents just loved him to death and were overjoyed when we visited. Even my brother, whom I had never been particularly close to, enjoyed seeing him and watching him play with Chico. He and Janae begged us to get together and bring Baxter so the dogs could play. Over the months, we became as close as adult siblings should be; it was a miracle!

Of course I was prejudiced, but it seemed to me that Baxter was quite a special little guy. Maybe, I thought, I should spread the joy somehow. I considered using him as a stud, and dollar signs started dancing around in my head. I actually waited to have him neutered much longer than I normally did with my other animals, to preserve this possibility. I did some research on what has to be done to have a certified stud and found you have to guarantee/certify every part of their body, from vital organs to kneecaps. Also, I did have a little experience, back when I was a teenager, with breeding my toy poodle. It didn't go so well, to put it mildly. Actually, that's how I ended up having two poodles. My female poodle only had one puppy...born caesarian on Christmas day...and I couldn't bear to part with the baby when she grew old enough to wean, despite the many expenses footed by my dad. Dear old Dad forbade me to ever try breeding my dogs again.

I didn't want another failure, so I gradually abandoned the idea. When Baxter kept insisting on marking his indoor territory, I finally decided to have him fixed. He didn't seem to hold it against me, but it didn't help. He kept on making those six-foot circles, on the carpet, but stud service was definitely out of the picture, forevermore.

Then I considered having him become a therapy dog. I knew it would just be a volunteer job, no income, but maybe he could bring joy to the elderly or seriously ill children. Then I remembered how hard it was in puppy kindergarten just to get him to sit and stay, and I knew that was a no go, too. So I decided I would just have to love him for the wonderful little companion he was and settled in for the long term.

Time had flown, and he was already eighteen months old, full grown, and weighed all of seven pounds. He no longer looked like a puppy, though people still mistook him for one because of his small size. He now had beautiful humanlike hair that hung nearly to the floor, and his nose had matured into a nice solid black. I was very proud of him and took him out whenever I could. It must have been the stage of my life, but I was enjoying this little dog more than I could ever remember enjoying any of my pets. Terry and I were still ecstatic with our decision to indulge ourselves. Baxter had rekindled our love for each other and brought fun and excitement back into our marriage, after two decades of working and raising kids. Actually, he was the light of our lives, and since he was still just a pup, we were looking forward to the many years of fun and companionship that were still ahead for us.

Picture Section

♦ ♦ ♦

♦ ♦ ♦

♦ ♦ ♦

Chapter Eleven

On May 5, 2006, I had an early-morning dentist appointment. Baxter got up with me but thought it much too early to be up and around. So he chose to jump up on the couch and sleep some more while I got ready to go. He looked so cute curled up there, on his blanket, I didn't have the heart to disturb him. So I let him sleep and left a note for Terry that he hadn't been outside yet. As I was backing out of the driveway, Terry poked his head out of the upstairs window and waved goodbye. He said he would take Baxter outside when he got downstairs.

I left a little early for the appointment and actually arrived before they opened. So I sat in my car for a few minutes, just thinking ahead to lunch (eating is always one of my favorite subjects!) I realized I hadn't turned on my cell phone yet, so I reached for it and switched it on, just in case Terry called with lunch plans.

As I sat there enjoying a silent moment of peace and quiet, someone came up and pounded on my driver-side window. I nearly jumped out of my skin when the pounding broke into my thoughts. It was Terry, and by the look on his face, it wasn't good. I'd only been there for a moment; he must have followed right behind me after I left the house. But why? Instinctively I knew something was wrong.

"What's wrong?" I said.

"Coyotes got Baxter," he managed to say through his anguish.

"Oooohhhh noooo!" I screamed. "Is he dead?"

"Yes." He nodded his head. "He is dead."

I jumped out of the car and reached for him. We stood there in our anguish, hugging and crying and sobbing. We stood together for several minutes, trying to squeeze away the pain, maybe reversing time, maybe finding it just wasn't true. But that didn't happen, and I had to find out more.

"I took him out to go potty, and they were waiting for him. He began barking at one, and chasing it. It ran away from him, and I thought he was going to be OK.

But there was another one hiding in the bushes, and he got Baxter . . . just like *that*!" And he snapped his fingers to demonstrate.

"I heard him yelp once, then nothing." Terry's voice was thick and emotional. He sobbed, then paused a bit to regain his composure.

"It happened in a flash. There wasn't anything I could do. I called for him to come, but he didn't listen. I chased after them, but my slippers came off and I was running barefoot through the thistles and blackberries. I just couldn't catch them." He cried.

"I'm sorry," he sobbed even more. "I'm sorry."

"I hate telling you. I didn't want to, but I had to. I tried your cell, but it wasn't on, so I just got in the car and followed you."

"I'm sorry," he said again and again. His pain was deep, and I felt sorry for him too.

"Did you see it happen?" I asked, my own voice breaking and emotional.

"Yes," he sobbed, and I felt horrible for him. I knew that this would haunt him for the rest of his life. My heart broke for him, as well as for myself and Baxter.

We stood there for many more minutes, just hugging and crying in the parking lot of the dentist's office. Anyone watching us would certainly have known something was very bad. I'm sure we drew stares and whispers, if there was anyone paying attention.

"Come home with me," he pleaded. "Please. I can't be home alone right now."

I was torn. It takes so long to get a dental appointment . . . There would be a fee if I didn't keep this one . . . Would I be able to endure the appointment given my emotional state? I didn't know what to answer. Then my thoughts turned back to poor Baxter.

"What did you do with his body?" I asked.

"I don't have it. They carried him away."

"You didn't get him back?" Suddenly I was panic-stricken.

"What if he isn't dead? What if he is suffering? What if he is trying to get back home and can't?" Finally, I had a sliver of hope to cling to. Maybe things would be OK.

"I have to go!" And I knew I wouldn't keep that appointment, no matter what the consequences were. I had to go home and look for Baxter. Terry said he would let them know at the reception desk, and I made a mad dash for home.

I cried all the way back home (a seven- or eight-mile drive). I'm sure I wasn't driving too well, but I made it home without any problems. By the time I got there, I had nearly convinced myself that it would be OK. That I would find him, and a vet would be able to repair him, and eventually he would be fine. Maybe a little altered, but alive. After all, Mom's small poodle was attacked by a big dog decades ago, and even though he needed major surgery, and a long, long recovery, he lived. He was a bit crippled, and never quite the same after that, but he lived. Surely Baxter would too. I vowed to love him, and take care of him, no matter what his condition. No matter what his needs.

I got out of the car and ran around the back to the potty spot. Strange, it looked just the same: nothing amiss, nothing different. It looked the same as it had looked for at least the last ten years, since it had been logged. The only change in the twenty-seven years we had been there.

I started walking toward the trees that remained, away from our house. I walked and walked, and called his name frequently. I found nothing, except Terry's slippers. They were about a hundred feet from our house, in the thistles, just as he said. He must have gone back into the house and put on some shoes and immediately left for the dentist's office. Or maybe he was actually barefoot there. I didn't notice.

I called and called. There was no sign of Baxter. I searched all over the immediate area for thirty minutes or so. When Terry got home, we both searched for him. I slowly began to realize he wasn't coming home. He wasn't alive. They probably carried him a long way off. It occurred to me what an irony the microchip turned out to be. It would not be of any help, and I would probably never find him. Those coyotes didn't care that he was registered and traceable. It made no difference to them. This was the first time I had ever had an animal microchipped and nationally registered, and it was all for nothing. Slowly, I began walking back to the house. My heart was breaking and I couldn't bear the pain. When I got back to the kitchen table, I sank into a chair, crumpled forward, and just cried for a long while.

After a while, the reality of losing Baxter began to sink in. He was such a large part of our world; how would I tell everyone that he was gone? I dreaded calling my family to give them the news. I knew they would take it as hard as I did. But it had to be done, and the sooner the better. I didn't want to put it off; I had to do it now. I picked up the phone and dialed my parents'.

"I've got bad news," I said.

"Uh-oh," my mom muttered.

"Coyotes got Baxter," I told them. "He is dead."

"Oh no!" They were both on the line, and they had the same response. Then all three of us went silent for several seconds as the news bit into our minds and hearts. I gave them a brief account of what happened but just couldn't go into detail. They said they were sorry and asked if there was anything they could do. Mom excused herself from the conversation and left Dad to finish up. I knew she was hurting, and I felt bad I had to put her through it.

After hanging up with them, I cried more. But I couldn't stop now. I called Holli, our daughter, and was forced to leave a voice mail. Then I went to the computer and e-mailed everyone in my address book who knew Baxter. My message was short. "Coyotes got Baxter this morning. We are devastated," it read. I just didn't have it in me to give the whole story to anyone right now.

Holli soon returned the call. She also knew instinctively that something was very wrong. When I told her the news, she said, "Oh my god, Mom. I'm so sorry. I'm coming over right now. I'll bring Cerberus [her Doberman] to see if he can pick up a scent."

When they arrived, the Doberman immediately did pick up a scent, and the two of them took off toward the trees. I asked her to bring back Baxter's collar if she found it. They weren't gone long before she called from her cell.

"We found what's left of him," she said. "They took him to their den and ate him. There's no sign of his collar, but all that is left is an eyeball, his tail, some unrecognizable internal organs . . ."

"Stop!" I wailed. "I don't want to know any more." It was just too painful for me.

"What do you want me to do?" Holli asked.

She had taken a plastic bag with her to put his body into, if she found it. So I told her to put what she found inside the bag, but not to tell her dad exactly what was inside. I wanted to spare him as much anguish as I could, and to this day, we've never discussed what she found. He discovered it only when he read it here.

Even though there wasn't much left, I wanted to go through the process of burying him. But I didn't want to witness the burial; it was just too painful. So she and Terry buried the bag on the hillside where we had put so many of our fallen furry friends. He was in good company. There were over a dozen dogs, cats, birds, bunnies, turtles, and such buried there. After all, twenty-seven years is a long time. There was even the opossum that we unsuccessfully attempted to nurse back to health after a bout with one of our larger dogs, many years ago.

They put Baxter next to Cougar and Orlando. Their graves were still fairly fresh, since we just recently lost both of them to old age. Oh, how I wished we were saying goodbye to Baxter because of old age. I know that when they die of old age, that is all I can ask for: that they have lived a full life, I have enjoyed them as much as possible, and it is their time. But this was different, very different. Baxter was still a pup, and his death was a total shock. Mom was right again: it really did hurt too much to lose them. The pain was horrible.

Chapter Twelve

Baxter was killed on a Friday morning, and we had a very rough weekend. A few days earlier, we made plans to go out for pizza and beer with some friends that night. At first, we thought we would try to keep the date. We thought it might be good for us—get our minds off it. But a few hours before we were supposed to leave, I knew I wouldn't be able to go. I was a basket case, and I was sick to my stomach. I called to make my apologies and was again forced to leave a message. I was so emotional; I could barely get the words out and make them understandable. The next day, they brought us flowers. She said it just broke her heart to listen to my message and hear me in so much pain.

I couldn't eat. All weekend I felt nauseous, and there were times I thought I would vomit, though I never did. It was several days before I could do anything more than pick at food and nibble a few small bites. I was also very shaky. My hands trembled continuously, and my knees felt weak and wobbly.

So this is what it felt like to lose something, or someone, you loved deeply. I didn't like it much. It hurt. It hurt like hell. And right after the pain of loss came the guilt. And I heaped huge, heavy loads of it on myself.

First, as I remembered the losses my friends and family had endured, I felt guilty for feeling this way over a *dog*. He was after all just a *dog*. My cousin, who graciously called to offer her condolences, lost an infant to SIDS about thirty-five years ago. I had to think of her loss. What could I say to her? This was just a *dog*. My neighbor mysteriously lost her adult son just a few months earlier. Terry, over the years, lost both of his parents. A best friend was widowed. On the TV news, there was the grandfather who accidentally backed over his granddaughter. Surely, all of these losses were harder to bare and must have been extremely painful. Suddenly, I felt renewed sympathy for all of them.

Losing Baxter was the most painful loss I have ever experienced. That definitely makes me one of the lucky ones. I've never lost a child, a spouse, a sibling, or a parent.

Baxter was just a dog. But regardless of the immense pain of those others, it still hurt, and I felt guilty for it.

Then there was the guilt of letting it happen: why didn't I know this would happen? Why didn't I see it coming? Why didn't I do a better job of protecting him? How could I have been so stupid? Idiots like me didn't deserve to have pets if they weren't going to take care of them and protect them from harm. I failed Baxter, and I was ashamed of myself. I was scum. I should be punished.

For days, I cried in the shower, or while driving, or during the night. I tried to hide it from Terry because he was hurting too. And I talked out loud to Baxter. I apologized for bringing him home. I told him I was sorry he got me for a mom. I told him I was sorry I didn't take better care of him. I asked him to forgive me. I told him I loved him, and asked him to please meet me at the Rainbow Bridge, despite my poor care of him. I only hope he will.

While my grief was hard enough, watching Terry's pain was difficult too. He would, every once in a while, just gasp, jump, and start crying. He was mentally reliving the ambush. I tried to help as much as I could, but I knew this was serious. It was a life-changing event.

"Maybe you, or even both of us, should seek counseling," I said. "This is bigger than anything we have ever experienced, and professional help would probably be good. We will find the money to pay for it somehow. It's important."

He said no. "I wouldn't be able to tell a stranger how horrible I feel. I just want it all to go away."

"Fat chance," was my response.

Over the next few days, we got some sympathy cards. Even a few for "loss of pet," which I didn't even know they made. Every one of them made me cry. We even got one from his veterinary office. I had to call the doggie sitter who worked there and let her know that she wouldn't be keeping Baxter for me during our upcoming beach trip after all, that coyotes got him. She said, "Why do they get all the good ones?" I must admit, I didn't know they did.

Everyone was very sympathetic. All of my family hurt for me, and for their loss as well. I felt so bad making my parents, my brother, and Janae hurt. I felt like I had forced Baxter onto them and had caused them pain as a result. Again, the guilt. My brother offered numerous times to give me money for another dog. He wanted us to go right out and buy another one. He said it would ease the pain. I just couldn't see it and refused his money. I wasn't sure I would ever get another dog. It did hurt too much to lose them. Grief. Besides, I couldn't take his money. Baxter's death was in no way his fault. It was mine. Pain. And Mom: she was hurting almost as much as I was. Since she and Dad no longer had any pets, she enjoyed Baxter immensely. I know she cried almost as much as I did, though she never admitted it. Again, guilt, guilt, guilt.

Then there were the people on the outer edges of our wanderings: the dog owners at the park where we walked, the bank tellers, the security guard, our accountant and his staff, the owners of the antique mall. Everyone asked, "Where is Baxter today?" And every time I had to tell someone he was gone, I deeply regretted making him such a popular public attraction.

I avoided most of them if I could. At the park, I did not want to see the labradoodle and his owner. I just could not find the strength to explain the ordeal to her. I jumped off the trail in order to avoid her and her dog. Most of the time, I did whatever I could to avoid having to tell the story. I wasn't always successful, of course, and there were the inevitable encounters. It wasn't easy. But the tale always ended with heartfelt sympathy from the inquirer, and a few escaped tears on my cheeks.

Also, we had taken many, many pictures of Baxter growing up. It was fun. We considered it our duty as good pet parents. Every time I saw him doing something cute, I would run for the camera to record it for all time. Terry did too. I was even guilty of e-mailing several of those pictures to family and friends, who probably didn't care an iota about them. But now, those pictures haunted me. Each time they came up on the screen saver of our computer that sat in the family room, they were like knife stabs to my heart. I soon removed every one I came across, everywhere. I didn't delete them, or throw them out. I just moved them to someplace where I wouldn't have to see them unwillingly and be forced to think about him. Seeing them simply hurt too much. Someday, if I wanted to see them again, they would still be there. Just not now.

Worst of all, I couldn't even pet another dog for a couple of weeks. And me, a lifelong dog lover. Someone who always had to stop and pet a dog and talk just a little bit with the owner. Me, whom Terry always got exasperated with, for delaying a hike or walk, just to pet a dog and chat a bit with its owner. I couldn't bring myself to touch a dog. It was just too painful. When I finally did pet a very calm and soothing standard poodle one day on a hiking trail, I wondered if he could feel my pain, if it was as obvious to him as it was to me. I stifled more tears as we parted on the trail, and he stopped and looked back at me for a moment. I do think he knew. Somehow.

Terry and I grew even closer after losing Baxter. We would talk into the night about how much we missed him. The bed seemed empty without his warm little body next to me. Sometimes we would remember some silly incident or mannerism that gave us a little chuckle, like his peculiar way of urinating. Or, when the pain was too great and one of us broke down, the other always offered comfort. It was wonderful to have someone who understood. Strange, even in death Baxter was bringing people closer.

Gradually, over the next few weeks, life began to return to normal. The tears became less and less, and the grief became bearable. The pain never went away completely—it still hasn't. But we started going out with friends and family again. We could come and go with complete abandon, never having to worry about how long we would be gone, or what to do with a pet. The king-size bed was surprisingly large enough now. But the house was quiet, empty, and lonely. Terry complained that when he would come home from work, I never met him at the door jumping and panting, with my tail wagging madly while trying to lick his face. I said it wasn't likely I would ever do that for him . . . no matter how much I loved him.

Eventually, we had the conversation about getting another dog. We both agreed that we didn't think we could live forever without a dog. That, eventually, we would want to get one, but not right now. It was too soon, too painful. And the dreaded question haunted us: what would we do about the coyotes?

Chapter Thirteen

Over the next months and years, I came to understand a lot about Mother Nature. Now I admit, most of this is pure speculation. I began to realize that the coyotes had always known about Baxter. Indeed, they most likely had known about all of our many pets over the years. We had simply just been lucky that none had fallen prey to them before. How our two cats survived for a total of twenty-six years is a mystery to me. All I know is that they spent a lot of time in trees, or under the deck. So they knew too. But one died of old age in the garage, and the other on the couch, so they definitely were not attacked by the predators. Probably, our larger dogs were safe from the coyotes, just by sheer size. Also, they were loud and rowdy, so if the coyotes were ever close, they must have been scared away quickly.

I'm pretty sure Baxter knew about the coyotes too. That's why he spent so much time sniffing around the property and bushes. That's why he wouldn't come when I called sometimes. It just smelled too interesting.

And how do the animals know so much? Urine. It's Mother Nature's identification card. The more I observed animals, and thought about it, the more it all fit. Now, I make no claim to being an expert. I hold no degrees in animal husbandry. And I am not a so-called animal whisperer. But I believe animals can tell a lot about another animal by the scent of the urine. They may even be able to judge the size of the animal, by the urine's placement on trees and bushes. A high level indicates a large animal. A small "puddle" or area of urine would suggest a small animal or a female.

I also believe they can tell the difference in urine from a squirrel, a mouse, a bird, a rabbit, or a deer. And I think that from this, the coyotes actually decide their hunting routes. I believe they had been gunning for Baxter for a while. We had just been lucky it didn't happen sooner. There had been some minor incidents, but we had simply been fortunate that they were unsuccessful.

Also, there was Christy, my little poodle who had disappeared just a few months after moving into our home, twenty-seven years earlier. The one who was the result of trying to breed my female when I was a teen. She was getting old. Terry always told me she was probably sick and went off to die alone. I had no other explanation, so I tried to believe him, but I was always skeptical. Maybe she just simply ran away and couldn't find her way back to the new house. I searched for her for weeks but never found so much as a trace. I had hoped someone was smitten with her and took her home and loved her. Now, I began to realize she probably had fallen prey to the coyotes too. It was just that no one witnessed the attack, so we were left to forever wonder. With Baxter, there was no doubt because Terry was by his side and saw the whole thing.

In addition, I came to realize that even if a person knew this could happen and was prepared, it is not possible for him to stop a coyote attack. You simply cannot run or react fast enough to intervene. It happened in the time it takes for a camera to flash. Nothing could have saved him. Even if Terry had had a loaded gun, ready to shoot, Baxter would still be dead.

Also, I began to think about our home and acreage. We had been there nearly twenty-seven years, and I was long comfortable with the safety of the setting and location. As I have said, we had dozens of pets over the years. What changed that put Baxter in jeopardy? Then it occurred to me: plenty!

When we first moved in, there had been heavy equipment, hammers, saws, and groups of workers on-site for the previous eight or nine months. It even took a while for the birds to return to the trees after we moved in. Everything had been scared away in the process of building. Then for many years, we had children, swings, toys, noise, activity, pets. All things contrary to the quiet woodsy setting it had once been. I'm sure the animals noticed.

Then, the kids began driving. There were cars in and out of the driveway constantly. With four adults working, going to school, participating in numerous activities and social events, our house was like Grand Central Station. We also liked to entertain and had many a backyard barbecue. Again, near constant noise and activity.

The eighty acres immediately behind our property had been logged when we were living there about seventeen years. We were told there was something like three-fourths of a million dollars' worth of timber there at the time. We were kind of sorry to see it go, but also liked the new openness, and we savored the sunlight. Previously, it was dark and damp; now it was bright and open. We even could see the sun and moon rise, which we considered to be a treat. But the new open space left less area for all the birds and critters. There was no longer shelter for them, and like the owls that once called the woods home, most moved on.

But in the ten years since being logged, the property had changed again. We didn't notice, but the animals did. The underbrush grew back, thick and heavy this time because of the new sunlight. And they repopulated the area. Also, we started feeding the birds and squirrels after the logging. We enjoyed watching them, but they filled in a couple of missing links in the food chain.

Both large and small animals made new homes and paths through the brush. That underbrush had not only given the coyotes a den to live in, but had hidden them on the morning of the attack. I believe they had a good idea of our routine and might have even been waiting for Baxter to come out. Maybe they were there several times before their plan worked. And this time they were successful.

Our property, which we took for granted for twenty-seven years, had slowly and subtly changed again recently. Since the kids left home several years earlier, it was just us two old poops, and it had grown silent again. No traffic, fewer parties, less noise, and the animals had reclaimed their territory. We didn't notice. Or rather, we didn't pay attention, until it was too late.

Again, I am not an expert on Mother Nature, or animal behavior. These theories are just my opinion. Maybe I am only rationalizing to make myself feel better. But by my observations, they seem to make sense. I believe there is a wealth of Mother Nature going on all around us humans. We just don't take the time to notice.

Chapter Fourteen

After losing Baxter, I hated the coyotes. I grew upset every time I saw one. Before, I had always found them interesting, and having a love for all nature, I tried to live peacefully beside them. We gently teased our son for being afraid of them when he was a boy growing up. I even enjoyed listening to their occasional howls during the night. No more. They did not return the favor. Even still, I realized they did not do anything wrong. They didn't know they ate my precious Baxter; they were only doing what comes naturally: surviving. To them, he was little more than a rabbit or squirrel.

A few people told me to poison them. Some volunteered to shoot them. But the truth is, I didn't want them dead, just gone. Away from my yard, my home, and my sight. I couldn't blame them for what they did. They are continually being squeezed out of their habitat by us ever-expanding humans. If they had to get more and more resourceful to find food, it was probably our own fault. No, they shouldn't have to die for that. Besides, what if the poison was eaten by the wrong animals, or worse, a child! What if someone "enjoyed" shooting them. That would have really bothered me. I can't understand killing animals for fun, and wanted no part of anything even remotely resembling revenge. I already had enough guilt to deal with, so I had to find another way.

I started thinking about Mother Nature herself. What would be the natural way to get the coyotes out of the area? Of course! Urine. It was the logical answer. But what were coyotes' natural predators? What would send them packing voluntarily?

I searched the Internet for answers and found cougar urine. Unbelievable! You could actually order many different kinds of urine and have it delivered to your door via the postal service. I was mildly shocked, but according to the ads, urine was used by farmers, hunters, trappers, and more to either attract or repel various animals. The ads said that farmers used it to protect newborn sheep and calves, and hunters and trappers used it to attract whatever species they were looking for. You could buy mountain lion (cougar) urine, buck urine, doe urine, bear urine, fox, raccoon, rabbit, mink, and yes, even coyote urine. Amazing! But I didn't even want to think about how it was collected.

I decided to order some cougar urine, coyotes' natural enemy. It was rather pricey at $50 a pint, and that was as much as I was willing to spend until I knew whether it would work or not. The directions said I just had to squirt it around the area I wanted protected, over a period of several days. I knew a pint wouldn't last long, but it was a start.

The website had an online order service, so I placed the order and waited. I must admit, I was a bit frightened by the prospect of playing Mother Nature myself. What if it actually *attracted* a cougar or cougars to our yard? I definitely did not want that; they would be a larger danger than the coyotes. Of course, there were no cougars in our area (except the mascot at the local university), but they were known to be in the county.

I rather thought of the urine as a potential for tipping the scales of nature to an unnatural balance, with far-reaching and perhaps long-range repercussions. What if it was sort of a pint-sized atom bomb in the animal kingdom? Could it yield that much power? I didn't need to worry. The company soon e-mailed me and informed me that they could not fill my order. It seems that selling cougar urine is illegal in the state of Washington. Hmmm. It had already been outlawed? Maybe I was right about that pint-sized atom bomb.

So I was back to square one. How could I naturally repel the coyotes? What could I use to mark the territory as mine, not theirs? My mind swirled, and before long, I remembered a movie we watched many years earlier called *Never Cry Wolf.* A great story about studying and living among wolves in the wilds of Alaska. In it, the main character observes the wolves marking their territory, and he decides to fight fire with fire, or rather, urine with urine. Thus, he begins marking *his* territory as well. And then it struck me, like a ton of bricks: I had my own territory-marking male right there, in my own household. My husband! And he worked for free!

Now, you may laugh, and I may live to regret admitting this, but I told Terry I wanted him to begin urinating all around our yard.

"As much, and as often as you can," I told him. "Start with the trails and paths that we've seen the coyotes using, and work around from there." Naturally, he was shocked at first, but after explaining what I discovered, he readily agreed.

He was always discreet, using the cover of darkness, or that underbrush I spoke of, so as not to be seen by any neighbors. And to my knowledge, he was never caught. We shared many a private joke about his "appointed rounds." The chuckles were plenty, but I think he actually took great pride in taking back his own territory. It was a job only he could do, and he did it to the best of his ability.

He continued with his duty all summer and into fall, until the weather got too nasty for him to be out there. We did tell a few trusted friends and family members what we were doing, but mostly it was a sacred secret between us. Those who knew agreed it was at least worth a try and, after the initial amusement, gave us their best wishes.

In addition to marking our territory, we blocked all known paths with trees, limbs, blackberry vines, and other debris so the coyotes had to at least make a detour. Also, though we didn't actually lay eyes on them often, when we did, we chased and shouted at them, making them run away, letting them know they were no longer welcome here. We also informed all the neighbors we knew to be careful, that their pets were in danger. We asked them to chase the coyotes away too, whenever they could.

It seemed like our plan to rid ourselves of the killers

was working. We actually saw and heard less and less of them over time. Something that was okay with me.

Chapter Fifteen

We went without a dog for about six weeks. The longest time I was without at least one dog since I was five years old. And it seemed very lonely. There was no one to greet us at the door when we got home, no doggie kisses, no one to cuddle up with on the couch. No one got excited when we went bye-bye. And no fuzzy friend sighed and curled up next to me in bed. With no pets, however, it was an easy, carefree life—no worries about how long we were gone from home, or where to find a shady parking spot for the car, or if dogs were allowed at our destination. But we didn't like it. We sorely missed canine companionship, and we wanted to numb the pain of losing Baxter. But were we ready?

I started secretly checking the newspaper ads, not telling Terry what I found. I wasn't sure if he was ready yet, and I didn't want to rush him. He had been through a lot, and I was willing to wait as long as necessary. I checked the ads any morning I had time. Sometimes I found an interesting ad, sometimes there were none. Occasionally, the puppies were listed as sold, or just not listed anymore, and I felt disappointed, as if I'd lost another one.

Late one morning, out of nowhere, Terry said to me, "There's a Papillon in the paper today for $299." I gasped and my mouth dropped open. I was stunned . . . he had been checking the ads too, but not telling *me*! We had secretly been protecting each other!

"I know," I said, after a brief moment of recovery. "I already looked."

We discussed calling on the ad, but I was scared. Were we really ready that quick? What if it happened again? What if this one got sick? What if we lost another one? What if . . . what if . . . what if . . . ? Those what-ifs seemed to pile up into a solid insurmountable wall. But we talked on and finally decided we were ready to try again. Making the loss of Baxter our last memory, after a lifetime of happy dog memories, was just too sad. We wanted another dog.

"You better call," he said.

"I don't think I can," I said. "I'll start crying."

So he picked up the phone and dialed the number. From his side of the conversation, and the voice I could hear coming through the line, I knew it was the same place where we got Baxter. And I knew instantly we would soon have a new puppy.

We made the arrangements to meet and started on our way, that same sixty-mile round-trip, though this time not at rush hour. In the car, I began to think about what we would tell the lady who was selling the puppies. It was Doris again, and it had been less than nineteen months since we bought Baxter. I knew she would recognize our names, maybe even remember us individually. What if she refused to sell me another puppy because I did not take good care of the first one? What if she scolded me for being so careless? I knew I would buckle under the pressure. What if she said since we lived in the same house and there was still the danger of coyotes, she wouldn't sell me another puppy and put it in danger? Again the what-ifs threatened to overtake us.

So we came up with a plan. We would tell Doris it was just a dog that attacked Baxter, not a coyote. I must confess, this is the first time in my life I planned to tell a little white lie. I have always been a very honest person, and I don't like the feeling of concocting an out-and-out lie. But I wanted another puppy. So I apologize, Doris. If you are reading this today, I am sorry for misleading you. I hope you understand.

When Terry and I walked into Doris's living room and peered into the playpen, this time corralling four puppies, our eyes grew large, and we both gasped. Again, there would be no question about which puppy to choose. For there, in that same real-life playpen, sat Baxter's identical twin. We looked at each other, pointed, and said simultaneously, "That one!"

But almost immediately, despite my best efforts, I began to cry. I tried to hide the tears, but they just wouldn't stop. My heart was breaking all over again from flashbacks of seeing Baxter in that very same playpen, just about nineteen months earlier. Terry asked Doris for a tissue, and that launched us into the story of why it made me cry.

"We got a dog from you last year," I said. "He looked exactly like this one, but he died." Oh, how I hated telling her. It tore me apart.

"What happened?" she asked softly, while handing me the tissue.

"It was no fault of yours. The puppy was perfect. He was killed by another dog."

There were more tears and an awful, painful lump in my throat, along with guilt from the lie.

"Oh, I am so sorry," Doris said. "I lost one that way too. Did you sue the owner?"

"No," I said. "It was just outside our property line, and he wasn't on a leash." Both true. "And, he started it." Also true.

"Well, you should have at least made them pay for the dog. That's what I did when it happened to me. They paid without question." She went on to tell the story of how a large dog just ran up and grabbed her small dog by the neck and killed it instantly. I couldn't tell her there was no one to sue, but I did tell her that was exactly what happened to Baxter, and that it happened in an instant.

"I was afraid you wouldn't sell me another after knowing what happened to the first," I told her.

"No," she said. "I can see that you loved the dog. And that you probably gave it a good home. Sometimes bad things happen. It isn't anybody's fault."

She was a very kind and compassionate person who also knew the love and loss of a dog. I was relieved, but those tears and that lump just wouldn't go away.

As we proceeded with the sale and registration papers, we began talking about how much this puppy looked like

Baxter. They were nearly dead ringers for each other. I told Doris I thought the name of his sire sounded familiar.

So we did some checking, and sure enough, the two dogs had the same father . . . they were half brothers! They never knew each other, of course. They had different mothers and were a year and a half apart, but brothers just the same. It somehow gave me a measure of comfort to realize that we were kind of getting back a piece of Baxter. Not just replacing him, but in a way, allowing him to live on. And in my mind, he would continue to be a part of our family. Needless to say, there were more tears.

For the second time in a little more than a year and a half, we finished with the care and feeding instructions of such a tiny puppy and headed off toward home. I think I cried most of the way. I was happy and fearful all at the same time. He was so cute. I was lucky to have him, but did I deserve him? Would this one make it? Would he live to a ripe old age? Would I be a better mother this time? For the next few days, my emotional state was all over the psychological charts.

I named our new baby Murphy. I didn't want Baxter 2, Baxter II, Baxter Jr., or anything to do with Baxter. I even thought of Advil because he would be such great pain relief. But this time, I knew how people are drawn to the breed, and I didn't want to have to launch into an explanation of how he got his name every time we met someone. I just came up with Murphy. I didn't even give Terry the chance for input. It was Murphy. That was that.

We decided to stop in at my parents' place before going home and let them in on the news. I was sure they would be excited for us since they too had been offering to help us buy another dog. I hid Murphy under my shirt when we walked in. He was tiny enough for them not to notice.

"We have a surprise," I said.

"You do? What is it?"

"We have a new puppy!" And I yanked him out and placed him before them. They were ecstatic and instantly began making a fuss over him. They were happy for us, and it showed. I sent up a little prayer that this time, it would go better, and I would never have to break their hearts again.

The next day, I took Murphy to meet Chico. They were fast friends in no time, but it was Janae who came up with the final version of Murphy's name. She kept saying, "Oh, Mr. Murphy . . . ," and I liked it. So it stuck, and he officially became *Mr. Murphy* . . . much to Terry's chagrin!

Chapter Sixteen

Of course, we instantly fell in love despite ourselves and soon were hopelessly attached to Mr. Murphy, just as we had been with Baxter. Before long, we found ourselves back in the familiar routines of potty-training, socializing, leash-training, and introducing him to his new life. Again, we quickly began walking him regularly and taking him with us wherever we went, whenever we could. Again, we got those same questions. And yes, we gave the same answers: Papillon. French. Butterfly wings.

A few months later, he and I went back to puppy kindergarten. We attended in a different location because I didn't want to have to explain to Debbie what happened to Baxter; it was still too painful. But things were much different this time around.

This time, I didn't want Mr. Murphy to just get by on his cuteness. I took his training seriously, and I needed him to also. I didn't give in as easily. When he failed to obey an important command, he got scolded more than Baxter ever did. We worked tirelessly, the two of us, on learning the lifesaving commands of "no!" and "sit!" and "stay!" I didn't want to go through the agony of losing another canine companion, so this time he had to mind me. Period.

And potty training was definitely different. We decided the danger was just too great to keep taking him outside, the way we had been doing since time immemorial. I would grow fearful just carrying Mr. Murphy outside in my arms. I even had frequent flashbacks of Baxter's attack, even though I didn't actually witness it. And I still couldn't bring myself to walk into that area of our property, so I had to come up with another way. I decided to paper-train Mr. Murphy. I heard of other people doing this when they lived in high-rises, so I wanted to give it a try. It seemed silly to have two acres and not put them to good use, but my decision was final. He would be a "paperboy."

We fenced off a small area in the garage and lined it with newspapers. After a while, I even brought in Baxter's tiny fire hydrant. It was painful to see it again, but I hoped it would help Mr. Murphy get the idea. Again, the hydrant didn't do much good. But the regular treats he got whenever he pottied on the paper did. It really didn't take very long before he was going pretty regularly on the paper. In fact, you had to be careful where you laid down the morning newspaper . . . you just might not be able to finish reading it!

I was far more careful with everything I did with Mr. Murphy. He did not have the freedoms that Baxter or any of our other pets had enjoyed. He never, but never, went outside on his own. He didn't go anywhere without being on a leash. He was not allowed to mingle with larger dogs, and he had to obey "sit," "down," and "stay." So we continued to practice them over and over and over. He did get to where he minded better than Baxter did, but in my mind, there will always be room for improvement.

Also, I did not make such a big deal about Mr. Murphy this time around. I didn't want the agony of having to tell dozens of people if the unthinkable did happen again. So this time, we kept the puppy more to ourselves. No more taking him into the accountant's office, or the bank, or friends' houses. He would just be our little treasure, not the world's. It made him a little more timid in the long run, and a bit more dependent on us for his security, but so far, it has been worth it. Hopefully, he will live much, much longer than his brother did.

Eventually, the three of us settled into a nice regular existence again, always making sure Mr. Murphy was safe. Always looking in full circles this time, not just straight ahead.

Chapter Seventeen

It has now been five years since we lost Baxter. In some ways, it feels like yesterday, and I don't think we will ever completely heal. But getting Mr. Murphy has helped ease the pain immensely. And MrM (my text name for him) is *so* much like Baxter, it's amazing sometimes. They remain nearly identical in appearance. I think only I can tell the difference in pictures, on the rare occasion that a picture of Baxter surfaces. Even Terry asks which is which occasionally.

And they have many of the same mannerisms: MrM also sleeps *under* the covers, right next to me, and he also gently scratches three times to get there. He too follows me everywhere . . . even into the bathroom. Like Baxter, MrM also loves toes, but also earlobes of all things! Like his half brother, MrM enjoys being as high up as possible, on sofa backs or shoulders, whenever he can; and he likes to be more vertical than horizontal when being carried. He chases and nips my feet when I walk barefoot, just as Baxter did. It's surprising how much those tiny little teeth can hurt! And he too is a very good communicator. Like his brother did, he uses his eyes, ears, voice, and paws to tell us exactly what he wants. He stares at me, whimpers, and makes little growly sounds, until I figure out that his food is stuck together, and he wants me to stir it for him. Or he paws my hand three times and sniffs the jar lid when he wants a drink of water while in the car. Sometimes Terry can figure out what he wants better than I can (guess it's a guy thing). And of course he loves to travel in the car and go for walks, but these traits are common to most dogs. As for beer, this time, I won't let Terry start it. But the dog does act as though he would take it, if offered.

However, there are a few differences too. Mr. Murphy does not have the dynamic personality that Baxter had. And maybe it's merely the result of my fears and overprotection, but Mr. Murphy is a much bigger chicken. He rarely challenges anything: cat, dog, or human. He takes off at the slightest hint of danger or noise, but that's okay with me.

He's not quite as sociable either. He is more timid and much less outgoing, more content to hang back and stay with us when in a crowd. He likes people and children OK but doesn't seem to need to be the center of attention as Baxter did. He also seems to be more of a lover, and less of a clown. But the biggest visible difference, of course, is how he urinates. Mr. Murphy squats, or lifts his leg, like a normal male dog. No front feet, no six-foot semicircles, no bobbing tail. It is rather, well, boring. Also, this time, I had him neutered when he was about four months old. So no pottying in the house either. Something else that's okay with me. Yes, Mom, I finally did spare those carpets.

Mr. Murphy is five years old now—much older than Baxter was when he died, and no longer a puppy. We didn't have the privilege of knowing Baxter at this age, so we can't compare. He definitely has gotten calmer and quieter than Baxter ever was. But of course, that is undoubtedly age related.

We have gone on several major trips with him, and he is a great traveler. At first, he seems to be a little confused by new surroundings, but then just settles in, goes with the flow, and is happy to be with us. In fact, I think he must love us as much as we love him, because he likes touching both of us at the same time, whenever he can.

Even though he isn't a puppy anymore, Mr. Murphy loves to play with his toys . . . one for his mouth and one for his feet, just like Baxter did. I couldn't bear to see or hear the Taco Bell talking Chihuahua again, so I threw out all of Baxter's toys, but Mr. Murphy doesn't try to make anything squeak, so he probably wouldn't have enjoyed it as much anyway.

Unfortunately, he has been diagnosed with that kneecap weakness (luxated patella) that the breeders try to screen for. His kneecap does pop out on occasion. But, when it does, he limps directly over to me, and I pop it back in for him. It is painful at times, but seems to be tolerable, though he will likely be on medication for it the rest of his life.

Our family loves Mr. Murphy as much as we do, though they still talk about Baxter now and then. Chico, the Chihuahua, now has a new little sister, Chiquita. And although she is a little hellion, it is fun to get the three of them together. Janae now has a "double" birthday party for Chico and Chiquita, and we call them all cousins and make family jokes about how they all party together. It's great fun.

Chapter Eighteen

In the five years since losing Baxter, our lives have changed dramatically. Hardly anything is the same. First, we moved from the family home where he was killed. We are twenty-two miles away in the small town of Kalama and have a gorgeous view of the Columbia River. It's the first time in my life I have lived outside of Clark County, and the farthest I've ever lived from where I was born! I can't say that losing Baxter was the only reason we left, but the heartbreaking memories certainly contributed to our decision to move on. We now live on a very small city lot, in an active neighborhood. We have deer, but no acreage, no trees, and no coyotes.

Terry has retrained Mr. Murphy to potty outside. Something I'm not too crazy about, but it seems to be working OK. He takes MrM for a short walk every morning, and we always carry a little bag to pick up after him. Occasionally, he is even allowed to wander within a tiny fenced area we've created for him under the deck. But he is never allowed out there unsupervised; I'm still too paranoid for that. Someday we hope to be able to fence the new backyard for MrM so he can have a little bit of the freedoms that Baxter and our other pets enjoyed. But for now, he doesn't know the difference, and he seems content.

Also, we sold the Baskin Robbins store in 2005, and I later got my real estate license. It is far more time-consuming (and far less profitable!) than the store was. This new career takes me away from home a lot. But Terry was forced into retirement with the slow economy, which leaves him home a lot. So we have sort of switched roles in caring for MrM and spending time with him. Terry does a good job, but I must admit, I am a bit jealous of the time they get to spend together.

Finally, both of the kids have switched marital status. Kyle married that LA girl in a beautiful ceremony in 2009, in San Francisco, her hometown. They lived in Boston for several years, but have recently moved back to the Los Angeles area. We don't get to see them much, but he calls and chats with us regularly. He's been away from home for twelve years, and I still miss him every day. Holli and

Jeff's marriage didn't survive, and they are enduring a painful divorce.

Losing Baxter was very difficult. Terry and I went through some rough times, but we are okay. One thing I am grateful for is that we never blamed each other. That's why our marriage not only survived, but was even strengthened by the ordeal. Because even the loss of "just a dog" can eat away at a relationship, until it too is lost. I blame myself for not realizing the danger, but Terry was just following standard procedure that fateful morning. In fact, all of our previous animals, cats and dogs alike, never had as much protection as Baxter did.

With all of them, for all the years we lived there, or anywhere, we would simply open the door and let them out. They would come back when they were ready. Sometimes it was hours, sometimes days, but they always came back. I decided early on that we needed to "escort" Baxter out, and Terry did that. How could either of us have known it would not be enough. No, I never blamed Terry, and he never blamed me. We accepted it was just "one of those things," and that helped us get through it.

Baxter was just eighteen months and ten days old when he died, and he lived with us for only seventeen months, but he touched our lives deeply. Losing him drew us closer together than we had ever been, in those thirty-one years of marriage. For me, it helped underscore that Terry is a good man, a good husband, and I am lucky to have him.

Mr. Murphy is a wonderful companion, and not surprisingly, we love him dearly. Even though he came to us through tragedy and loss, he is the new center of our world. To outsiders I'm sure we seem a bit silly at times. We both put his needs first before ours, just as we did with our kids. Always watching out for him. Always being overprotective. But despite everything we do, and our deep attachment to him, he can never erase the memories of Baxter.

Sometimes I wonder if there was even a bit of divine intervention, or cosmic fate, because Mr. Murphy was born two weeks before we ever knew we would need him. It seems he was always part of a larger plan, directed by someone much more powerful than myself.

But still, all things considered, it was a difficult decision to move forward and get another dog. It felt disrespectful to Baxter, and we were riddled with guilt and fear. Now, however, we can't imagine life without our Mr. Murphy and his little "butterfly wings." And this time, armed with new information and a renewed sense of vigilance, I hope and pray we won't have to for many, many years . . . after a full canine lifetime of love and companionship, from yet another *old* furry friend.

Because in the years since Baxter's death, I have come through with a new personal philosophy: dying of old age, is the *most* we can expect, from any living creature.

EPILOGUE

A Word to the Wise

The tragedy that unfolded in these pages is a true story and, unfortunately, all too common. Coyotes are found throughout North America, and there are tens of thousands of them in the state of Washington alone. Humans are intruding into their habitat, making them less wary of people. The U.S. Department of Fish and Wildlife has no specific figures but says attacks are on the rise. Since most go unreported, it is possible that thousands of pets are attacked or killed each year by coyotes in the United States. It *can* happen to you. But if you are prepared and follow some simple precautions, you can reduce the risk of losing your four-footed friend to their wily ways. Here are some tips that may help protect you:

- If you have seen or heard them, coyotes are there. Do not assume they have moved on. Chances are, they have made a home in the area and will remain for a long period of time.

- All small pets, dogs and cats alike, are easy prey for coyotes. Don't leave food or water outside that might attract the predators or their prey. Also, this seems to go without saying, but never feed coyotes. They will not only become accustomed to humans and their pets but will get aggressive if food is withheld. I emphasize, they are *not* pets, but rather, wild animals whose only job is to survive.

- Coyote packs are a big danger. In general, packs form when a breeding pair is feeding new pups and are especially troublesome in spring. One coyote will flush out their game, while the other hides in bushes or tall grass and waits to make the surprise attack. They will then return to their den and share the food. I believe this is exactly what happed to Baxter.

- Do not feed birds or squirrels on the ground. Keep feeders elevated and clean up any spilled seed as coyotes can be drawn to the seeds, or to the birds and rodents who eat them. Pick up any fallen fruit from fruit-bearing trees as it too is bait for the small animals that coyotes eat.

- Keep ground covers and low vegetation trimmed around areas frequented by your pets and children. Not only can they hide a coyote, but can attract as well the rabbits, squirrels, and rodents that coyotes eat. Keeping all links in the food chain close by.

- Keep all small animals indoors or on a leash. Do not assume you can prevent the attack if you are close. It is not physically possible for humans to react or run fast enough to stop a coyote attack. They can jump, attack, and crush a small animal's neck in one swift move. It only takes a split second. Even if you are able to chase away the coyote and get your pet back, chances are it will already be dead or will not survive the attack.

- Don't leave small animals unattended, even in a fenced yard. Coyotes are known to climb or jump fences, or dig underneath to get to prey inside. Put a cover on kennels or exercise yards for positive safety.

- If you see a coyote in the area, use noise and movement to scare it away. Yell, wave your arms, run, bang, rattle something, or throw rocks in its direction to make it run away. Best advice if you see a coyote close by: pick up your furry friend and leave!

- Remember, it is not only coyotes that pose a risk to pets. Owls, eagles, and red-tailed hawks are also a very real threat, as well as cougars, wolves, and even bears, if they are in your area.

Also, and most importantly, not only small pets are in danger. It is rare, but small children have been attacked and badly injured or killed by coyotes and other predators. Don't take any chances. Baxter was just a dog, but losing a child would be unbearable.

CPSIA information can be obtained at www.ICGtesting.com
Printed in the USA
BVOW032349220212

283490BV00004B/1/P